Lerner SPORTS

SUPER SPORTS TEAMS

INSIDE THE ST. LOUIS CARDINALS

JON M. FISHMAN

Lerner Publications ◆ Minneapolis

Lerner Publications Company
An imprint of Lerner Publishing Group, Inc.
241 First Avenue North
Minneapolis, MN 55401 USA

For reading levels and more information, look up this title at www.lernerbooks.com.

Main body text set in Aptifer Slab LT Pro / Typeface provided by Linotype AG.

Designer: Kimberly Morales

Library of Congress Cataloging-in-Publication Data

Names: Fishman, Jon M. author.
Title: Inside the St. Louis Cardinals / Jon M. Fishman.
Description: Minneapolis: Lerner Publications, [2022] | Series: Super sports teams (lerner sports) | Includes
    bibliographical references and index. | Audience: Ages 7–11 | Audience: Grades 2–3 | Summary: "Dive deep into
    the world of the St. Louis Cardinals. From the team's origins to their defining moments, readers will discover
    why so many fans cheer for the Cardinals"—Provided by publisher.
Identifiers: LCCN 2021014959 (print) | LCCN 2021014960 (ebook) | ISBN 9781728441757 (library binding) |
    ISBN 9781728449494 (paperback) | ISBN 9781728445229 (ebook)
Subjects: LCSH: St. Louis Cardinals (Baseball team)—Juvenile literature.
Classification: LCC GV875.S3 F469 2022 (print) | LCC GV875.S3 (ebook) | DDC 796.357/640277866—dc23

LC record available at https://lccn.loc.gov/2021014959
LC ebook record available at https://lccn.loc.gov/2021014960

Manufactured in the United States of America
1-49930-49773-8/23/2021

TABLE OF CONTENTS

Allen Craig smashes a home run during the 2011 World Series.

NUMBER 11

FACTS AT A GLANCE

- The Cardinals joined the **NATIONAL LEAGUE (NL)** in 1892.

- **BOB GIBSON** won three games in the 1967 World Series.

- **THE CARDINALS** won the World Series 11 times, second most in Major League Baseball (MLB).

- In 11 seasons with the Cardinals, **ALBERT PUJOLS** hit 445 home runs.

The St. Louis Cardinals were in big trouble in Game 6 of the 2011 World Series. They trailed the Texas Rangers 7–4 in the eighth inning. Texas had already won three games in the series. If they won Game 6, they'd be MLB champions.

Cardinals right fielder Allen Craig blasted a home run to make the score 7–5. In the ninth inning, Texas closer Neftali Feliz struck out two St. Louis batters. The Cardinals were down to their final out. David Freese batted with two runners on base. He smacked a triple to right field to tie the game!

St. Louis fans went wild with excitement. But their joy didn't last long. In the 10th inning, Josh Hamilton hit a two-run home run to give Texas a 9–7 lead. The Cardinals needed another comeback. This time, they hit three singles to add two runs and tie the score again.

Game 6 headed to the 11th inning. Freese stepped to the plate. After battling to a full count, he swung and crushed the ball. It sailed over the center field fence for a game-winning home run. The crowd roared, and fireworks exploded as Freese ran around the bases.

The next day, St. Louis won Game 7 and the World Series. Freese won the series Most Valuable Player (MVP) award. The victory was their 11th championship and proved once again that the Cardinals were one of MLB's greatest teams.

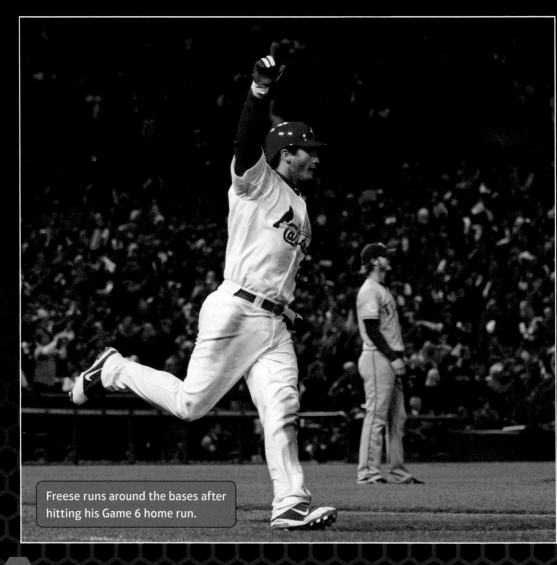

Freese runs around the bases after hitting his Game 6 home run.

Cardinals players celebrate
winning the 2011 World Series.

Rogers Hornsby helped the Cardinals win the 1926 World Series.

A WINNING TEAM

In 1882, the St. Louis Brown Stockings began playing in the American Association (AA). The AA was a pro baseball league that included six teams. The Brown Stockings finished in fifth place.

St. Louis shortened their nickname to the Browns the following year. They won the AA championship four years in a row from 1885 to 1888. In 1892, after 10 seasons in the AA, St. Louis joined the NL. Facing better teams, the Browns struggled. They had losing records in each of their first seven seasons in the NL.

The 1885 St. Louis Browns

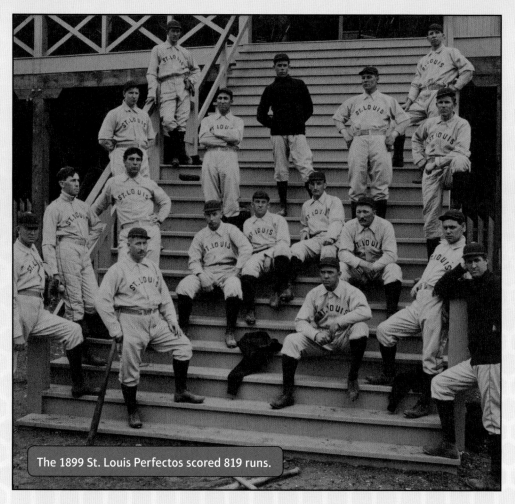

The 1899 St. Louis Perfectos scored 819 runs.

The team made another name change in 1899 to become the St. Louis Perfectos. That year, they finished with an 84–67 record, good enough for fifth place in the 12-team NL. But that didn't keep them from making more changes. In 1900, they became the St. Louis Cardinals.

In 1901, the American League (AL) became a major league equal to the NL. Two years later, the leagues combined to form MLB. The AL champion Boston Americans beat the NL's Pittsburgh Pirates in the first World Series in 1903.

It took St. Louis 23 seasons to reach their first World Series. Led by NL MVP Bob O'Farrell, the 1926 Cardinals had the best record in the league at 89–65. They faced the mighty New York Yankees in the World Series. St. Louis crushed New York 10–2 in Game 6 to set up a thrilling Game 7.

Rogers Hornsby (*bottom center*) touches home plate for the Cardinals while teammate Jim Bottomley (*top center*) follows in the 1926 World Series.

Hall of Fame pitcher Pete Alexander had many amazing moments with the Cardinals.

AMAZING MOMENTS

The Cardinals have had a lot of amazing moments. One of the earliest came in Game 7 of the 1926 World Series. Pete Alexander had already pitched 18 innings in the series and won two games for St. Louis. But with the Cardinals leading the Yankees 3–2 in the 7th inning, the team called on him again.

Alexander pitched two scoreless innings. Then, with just one out remaining for the Yankees in the final inning, Babe Ruth batted for New York. Ruth was the greatest player in MLB. No one had ever come close to matching his power with a bat. He had hit a home run earlier in Game 7.

Alexander pitched carefully to Ruth. He didn't want to throw a ball over the middle of home plate that Ruth could crush. Ruth soon drew a base on balls and walked to first base.

Babe Ruth jogging to home plate after hitting a home run in Game 7 of the 1926 World Series

Ruth wasn't known for his speed, but he suddenly took off running for second base. St. Louis catcher Bob O'Farrell threw the ball to second. Ruth was out! The wild play ended the World Series and gave the Cardinals their first title.

In 1928, the Cardinals again faced the Yankees in the World Series. This time, New York swept St. Louis in four games. The Cardinals won titles in 1931 against the Philadelphia Athletics and in 1934 against the Detroit Tigers. In 1942, St. Louis had another chance to take down New York in the World Series.

The Yankees won Game 1. St. Louis responded by winning the next three. In Game 5, the teams fought to a 2–2 tie. In the ninth

Cardinals outfielder Joe Medwick slides into third base during Game 7 of the 1934 World Series.

inning, Whitey Kurowski batted for the Cardinals. The 24-year-old rookie had hit just nine home runs that season. But with one runner on base, he was ready. He smacked a homer to left field to give St. Louis the lead. New York couldn't catch up, and the Cardinals had their fourth title.

In 1967, Cardinals pitcher Bob Gibson dominated the World Series. He allowed just one run to the Boston Red Sox to win Game 1. In Game 4, he didn't allow any runs and won again. Then he pitched nine innings in Game 7 to win a third time. Gibson also hit a home run to help his team win 7–2.

The Cardinals were back in the World Series the next year. They lost to the Tigers, but fans will never forget the way Gibson pitched in the Game 1 win. He struck out 17 Detroit batters. Gibson still holds the all-time World Series record for strikeouts in a game.

CARDINALS FACT

In 2011, Albert Pujols became the third player to hit three home runs in a World Series game. He joined Babe Ruth and Reggie Jackson.

Gibson follows through on a pitch during the 1967 World Series.

Mark McGwire launches his 62nd home run in 1998.

On September 8, 1998, Cardinals first baseman Mark McGwire smashed a line drive over the left field wall. The homer was McGwire's 62nd of the season, beating Roger Maris's record that had stood for more than 35 years. But he didn't stop there. McGwire finished the season with a shocking 70 big flies.

Although David Freese was the hero and MVP of the 2011 World Series, St. Louis first baseman Albert Pujols may have played the best game in World Series history. In Game 3, Pujols hit a single in the fourth inning and another in the fifth. In the sixth, he hit a home run. Then he hit another big fly in the seventh. Pujols came to bat again in the ninth inning with his team way ahead. He crushed yet another homer to help St. Louis win 16–7.

Pujols ranks fifth on MLB's career home run list.

Paul Goldschmidt is a Cardinals superstar. He has almost 300 career home runs.

CARDINALS SUPERSTARS

Cardinals history is packed with incredible players. In the 1920s, Rogers Hornsby was one of the top power hitters in the game. In 1926, he became St. Louis's full-time manager. He continued playing second base and led the Cardinals to victory in the World Series.

Many fans consider Stan Musial to be the greatest Cardinals batter. Musial played 22 MLB seasons from 1941 to 1963, all of them with St. Louis. He holds Cardinals records for home runs, hits, runs scored, and many more. He won three World Series titles and three NL MVP awards.

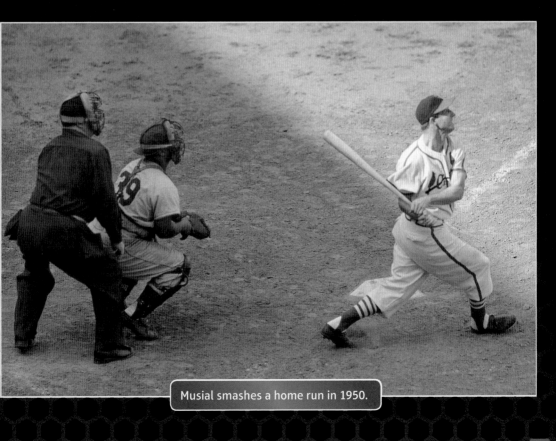

Musial smashes a home run in 1950.

No Cardinals pitcher can match the stats of Bob Gibson. He won 251 games in 17 seasons with St. Louis. Gibson won two World Series titles and was named series MVP both times.

Gibson threw 56 shutouts, or games when he pitched at least nine innings without giving up a run.

Ozzie Smith leaps over a runner to throw the ball to first base in 1996.

Ozzie Smith might be the most exciting player in Cardinals history. His amazing defense at shortstop is unmatched. The Wizard of Oz played for St. Louis from 1982 to 1996. During that time, he won 11 Gold Glove awards as the best defender at his position.

Yadier Molina throws to first base for an out.

Albert Pujols hit 445 home runs for the Cardinals from 2001 to 2011. In 2012, he joined the Los Angeles Angels. If he had stayed in St. Louis, he would have passed Musial's 475 and became the team's all-time home run leader.

New stars keep stepping up for St. Louis. Catcher Yadier Molina has won nine Gold Glove awards. Only two other catchers have won more. First baseman Paul Goldschmidt joined the Cardinals in 2019. He blasted 34 big flies that year to lead the team.

In 2021, the Cardinals made a huge deal. They traded five players to the Colorado Rockies for Nolan Arenado. The superstar third baseman averaged almost 30 homers a year for the Rockies. He also won the Gold Glove award eight years in a row.

Arenado is known for his big hits.

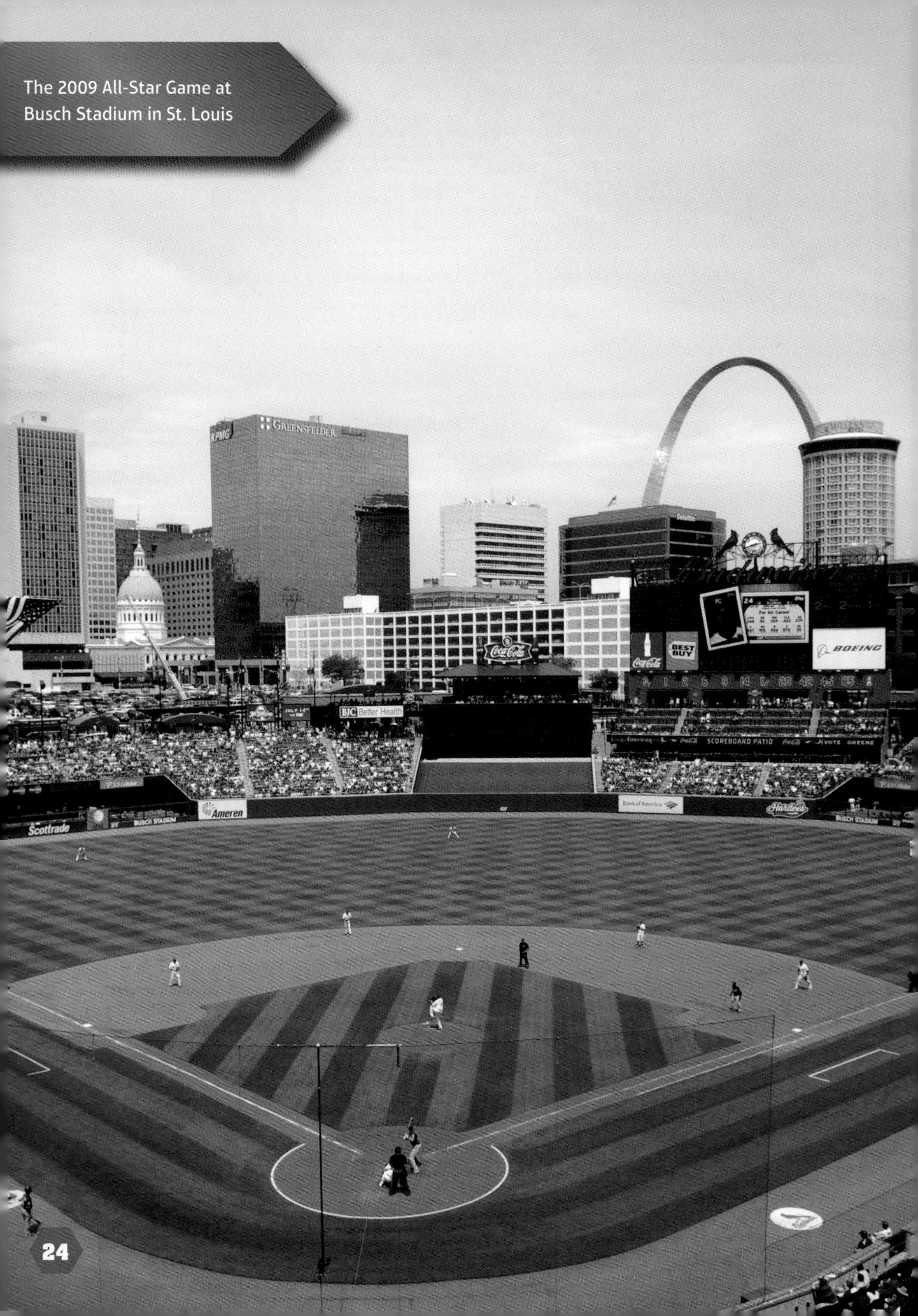

The 2009 All-Star Game at Busch Stadium in St. Louis

EXPECTING GREATNESS

Before 1922, the fronts of Cardinals jerseys were blank or had Cardinals, St. Louis, or St. L on them. That year, the team began playing with a new design. A baseball bat extended through the C in Cardinals, with images of cardinals perched on both ends of the bat. Modern St. Louis uniforms look much as they did in 1922.

Over the past 130 years, the team's stadiums have gone through a lot of changes. Between 1892 and 1952, the team played in four different home ballparks. In 1953, Busch Stadium opened in St. Louis. The team played there until 1966, when the second version of Busch Stadium opened.

St. Louis uniforms feature cardinals sitting on a bat.

In 2006, the team began playing in a brand-new Busch Stadium. The ballpark in downtown St. Louis can hold about 46,000 Cardinals fans. That year, the team won their 10th World Series. They became the only team to win the World Series in the first season of a new stadium since the Yankees did it more than 80 years earlier.

The Cardinals have appeared in the World Series 19 times. Their 11 World Series victories rank second in MLB behind the Yankees. St. Louis's history of success puts a lot of pressure on the team. Fans expect them to be good every season and compete for another World Series title. Modern stars like Yadier Molina, Nolan Arenado, and Paul Goldschmidt know that playing for St. Louis is an honor. They're ready to carry the team to their next World Series victory.

Cardinals fans cheer for their team, eager for another championship.

Cardinals players celebrate after winning their 11th World Series.

Albert Pujols

CARDINALS
SEASON RECORD HOLDERS

HITS

1. Rogers Hornsby, 250 (1922)
2. Joe Medwick, 237 (1937)
3. Rogers Hornsby, 235 (1921)
4. Stan Musial, 230 (1948)
   Joe Torre, 230 (1971)

HOME RUNS

1. Mark McGwire, 70 (1998)
2. Mark McGwire, 65 (1999)
3. Albert Pujols, 49 (2006)
4. Albert Pujols, 47 (2009)
5. Albert Pujols, 46 (2004)

STOLEN BASES

1. Arlie Latham, 129 (1887)
2. Lou Brock, 118 (1974)
3. Charlie Comiskey, 117 (1887)
4. Vince Coleman, 110 (1985)
5. Vince Coleman, 109 (1987)
   Arlie Latham, 109 (1888)

WINS

1. Silver King, 45 (1888)
2. Dave Foutz, 41 (1886)
3. Bob Caruthers, 40 (1885)
4. Silver King, 35 (1889)
   Tony Mullane, 35 (1883)

STRIKEOUTS

1. Jack Stivetts, 289 (1890)
2. Dave Foutz, 283 (1886)
3. Bob Gibson, 274 (1970)
4. Bob Gibson, 270 (1965)
5. Bob Gibson, 269 (1969)

SAVES

1. Trevor Rosenthal, 48 (2015)
2. Jason Isringhausen, 47 (2004)
   Lee Smith, 47 (1991)
4. Trevor Rosenthal, 45 (2014)
   Bruce Sutter, 45 (1984)

GLOSSARY

base on balls: an advance to first base awarded to a baseball player who takes four pitches that are outside of the strike zone

big fly: a home run

closer: a relief pitcher who usually finishes games

full count: when the count to the batter is two strikes and three balls

line drive: a baseball hit in a nearly straight line usually not far above the ground

pro: short for professional, taking part in an activity to make money

rookie: a first-year player

shortstop: the player who defends the infield area on the third-base side of second base

single: a base hit that allows the batter to reach first base safely

triple: a base hit that allows the batter to reach third base safely

LEARN MORE

Doeden, Matt. *G.O.A.T. Baseball Teams.* Minneapolis: Lerner Publications, 2021.

Kelley, K. C. *St. Louis Cardinals.* Mankato, MN: Childs World, 2019.

Lajiness, Katie. *St. Louis Cardinals.* Minneapolis: Big Buddy Books, 2019.

MLB
https://www.mlb.com/

National Baseball Hall of Fame
https://baseballhall.org/

St. Louis Cardinals
https://www.mlb.com/cardinals

INDEX

PHOTO ACKNOWLEDGMENTS

Image credits: REUTERS/Jim Young/Alamy Stock Photo, p. 4; REUTERS/ Jeff Haynes/Alamy Stock Photo, pp. 6, 17; AP Photo/Matt Slocum, pp. 7, 27; Bettmann/Getty Images, pp. 8, 11, 14, 20; The State Historical Society of Missouri, p. 9; Library of Congress (LC-DIG-ppmsca-18777), p. 10; AP Photo, p. 12, 19; The Stanley Weston Archive/Getty Images, p. 13; Focus On Sport/ Getty Images, p. 15; AP Photo/Amy Sancetta, p. 16; AP Photo/Jeff Roberson, p. 18; AP Photo/Mary Butkus, p. 21; AP Photo/Tom Gannam, p. 22; Rich Schultz/Getty Images, p. 23; Gino Santa Maria/Shutterstock.com, p. 24; Rick Ulreich/Icon Sportswire/AP Images, p. 25; AP Photo/Mark Humphrey, p. 26; John Grieshop/MLB/Getty Images, p. 28.

Design element: Master3D/Shutterstock.com.

Cover: Jared Wickerham/Getty Images.